Crescendo Publishing Presents

Instant Insights on...

EMPOWERMENT

PERFORMANCE POWER:
Clarity, Confidence, & Joy

Molly Mahoney

small guides. BIG IMPACT.

Instant Insights on...

PERFORMANCE POWER: Clarity, Confidence, & Joy
By Molly Mahoney

Copyright © 2016 by Molly Mahoney
Cover Design by Melody Hunter

ISBN: 978-1-944177-43-0 (p)
ISBN: 978-1-944177-44-7 (e)

Crescendo Publishing, LLC
300 Carlsbad Village Drive
Ste. 108A, #443
Carlsbad, California 92008-2999

www.CrescendoPublishing.com
GetPublished@CrescendoPublishing.com

What You'll Learn
in this Book

Have you ever wished you could summon the confidence of a Broadway performer? Would you like to walk into any situation and take command with a fearless sense of clear, focused determination? Would you like to present yourself with a contagious, positive energy, leaving others begging for an encore? You can! After years of performing in NYC, Las Vegas, regional theaters, and on cruise ships, Molly Mahoney has taken all that she has learned as a performer and reformatted it into a teachable system for business owners and professionals.

This system will give you the power to attack your goals and wow your clients with clarity, confidence, and joy. This boost of performance power is the perfect polishing touch for connecting with others and making a real impact, from your first impression to every connection you make along the way. After experiencing a boost of Molly's "performance power," you'll bring a newfound sense of stage presence with you as you take your own "show" on the road.

In this book, you'll get *Instant Insights* on...

- Unlocking your "inner awesome" and exude confidence so that you actually look forward to speaking in public

- Bringing more joy into your life every day so that you look forward to the morning alarm rather than dreading it

- Clarifying what you want and how to get it—after all, it's hard to achieve your goals if you don't know what they are.

- Dressing for success and how to make wardrobe choices that will lead you to a happier, more effective life

- Attacking every day as if you are stepping out into your own spotlight so that you can build an audience that loves you

- Developing a "polished plan" so that you can take your show on the road

A Gift from the Author

The Mini Performance Power Boost is a four-part video course that will enable you to bring a sense of stage presence to your everyday life so that you can fill your world with more clarity, confidence, and joy. Plus, you'll receive worksheets that will help you create a polished plan as you attack your goals, bringing to light the success that you deserve.

Access your gift here:
www.PerformancePowerBook.com

Table of Contents

Dedication

This book is dedicated to all the courageous performers who have opened their hearts and shared their voices with me as a coach and musical theater teacher. I'm a better teacher, a better coach, a better mom, and a better human because of you all. In the transformations you have made, you have helped me to see the power of connecting with your unique superpowers. Because of you, I am able to share those secrets with business owners and their teams. Because of you, I live a life full of magic and joy. Because of you, that magic and joy has been translated into a movement that I'm beyond proud to be leading.

Thank you for your joy. Thank you for your courage. Thank you for your song.

The Key to Confidence

What if I told you I knew the secret to feeling fearless in any situation? What if you could posses the key to pure power in any moment? What if you could summon a crazy sense of confidence that would enable you to fill a room with goodness and leave others begging for more?

As you may have guessed, you can.

As a young performer hitting the NYC audition scene, I found myself falling lower and lower as I went into audition after audition without actually landing a job. I was like countless other young actresses who pour their hearts and souls into their dreams: wide-eyed, bursting with talent, and hungry to please.

Then it all shifted.

I went to what is called an Equity Chorus Call (ECC), an audition where members of the Actors Equity Association (a union for stage actors) are guaranteed a chance to audition for a spot in a performance. At the time of this audition, however, I was not a union member. I was trapped with the other budding performers in a long, narrow hall outside the audition lounge, surrounded by women who were taller, thinner, younger, older, just … "–er" than me.

Sometimes these auditions lasted all day— literally eight hours spent sitting on the floor or a little bench trying to stay fresh for the two-minute make-or-break moment of your life that ended with a simple, "I'm sorry. We won't have time to see you today."

Are you kidding me?

No, I'm not.

This particular day we had been waiting for about three hours when I needed to use the restroom. I went to the woman at the front desk and muttered politely, "Excuse me, where would I find the restroom?" The woman at the desk looked at me, raised one eyebrow, and said, "If you go downstairs, out the front door and to the right, you'll find a McDonald's in Times Square."

Uh ... what!?

"I'm sorry?" I said. "I'm here for the audition."

"Do you have an Equity Card?" she replied.

"No, but I'm here to audition," I smiled.

"You can go to the McDonald's in Times Square," she reiterated with a straight face.

I turned around and stared into the faces of twenty to thirty young, desperate girls, picked up my giant bag that held my jazz shoes, tap shoes, character heels, audition book filled with sheet music and headshots/resumes, and food for the day spent trapped in the hall, and went back to my 400-square-foot apartment.

What on earth was I doing with my life? Spending endless hours waiting for a two-minute shot at a job? Walking into a room and begging for the chance to be seen? As I walked down those stairs, I knew something had to change.

And it needed to change *now*.

What was it that was stopping us from booking work? From being seen in these auditions? Suddenly, it all became clear.

When I walked into these auditions, I was trying to impress, to be what they needed in their production, to guess what they were looking for, and I was doing everything possible to be just that—to do the impossible. There was only one thing I could be more of that would actually improve my shot at booking a show.

Maybe you've found yourself in a position like this. Maybe you've wondered why you aren't finding the success you know you deserve. You've worked tirelessly to achieve a promotion or a goal or a feeling of success and freedom, and yet you are still sitting in that narrow hallway, using the restroom at possibly the shadiest spot in Manhattan, unable to break through.

There is one thing that you can bring with you that will change your feelings of doubt and the way you are affecting the "casting directors" in your life.

That thing is you.

Yep! **YOU** are the secret to your success.

Not just the you who is begging for the job or promotion or newfound freedom in life. The you who is filled with an unbelievably unique sense of awesome.

Before you start to challenge me, before you throw out the first "yeah, but ..." I want to be very clear. Everyone has something that makes them uniquely awesome, even if it's just the fact that they make an amazing quesadilla.

I needed to stop trying to be what "they" wanted in auditions and be more of what I already was. I made a concerted effort to spend every day celebrating what makes me awesome and what filled me with joy (my own quesadilla recipe), *and* I began to search out and celebrate what makes others uniquely amazing as well. And do you know what happened? I started booking work like a mad woman. I earned my union card and booked show after show, including a national tour and a long stint at a regional theater that eventually brought me to my husband.

You can do this too! If you firmly commit to unlocking and celebrating what makes you awesome, you'll find the same shift in your life.

Start by making a list of *all* the things that make you awesome. If it's hard at first, don't worry. This is an ongoing list to which you can keep adding. These can be character traits that you possess, as well as things that give you that bubbly feeling in your chest, that fill you with joy.

As you head into each day, each meeting, each situation, you should lead with those things. No, you don't need to walk into a room and say, "Hi! I'm Susan and I love Brussels sprouts!" But you might want to look over that list and recall the way Brussels sprouts make you feel. Or maybe your quesadilla of awesome is made up of knitting, or skiing, or helping others. Once you've connected with your awesomeness, bring those things to the front of your energy, hold them in your chest, and beam them out like rays of sunshine.

Then—and this is the best part—recognize that there are things that make every person you meet equally awesome. They have their own quesadilla recipe that fills their chest with bubbles. They may not be aware of it yet, but if you can focus on finding their quesadilla and celebrating it, the energy in the room will shift. You'll draw in others who have more in common with you, enabling you to connect in business and in personal relationships. Another bonus? You'll stop comparing yourself. By celebrating their awesome, you give your inner glow a chance to burn a little brighter.

Your Instant Insights...

- Find your quesadilla—the things that make you uniquely awesome.

- Celebrate your awesome in everything you do.

- Recognize that others are filled with their own special blend of awesome and celebrate them.

#SpreadJoy

Finding your "quesadilla," recognizing your awesome, is the first step. So now you have a list of these qualities, hobbies, and bits of goodness that set you apart from others, but how do you ensure that those qualities live at the front of your life, that you lead with them every day?

It's simple really. You have to make the choice. You have to choose to commit to joy in every situation.

Performers are pushed to crazy limits. We're forced to live in and out of hotel rooms, wear crazy costumes, literally bleed for our art … and we do it anyway.

Why?

Because we have a crazy commitment to the dream. "The show must go on!" has been beat into us since our first childhood theatrical experience. There is no other option.

If you want a life and a business filled with clarity, confidence, and joy, you have to make the choice to commit to that dream *every day*.

Luckily, there are a few ways to enforce that commitment.

- **Recognize the joy that exists *every day*, and keep a record of it.** You can do this in a "joy journal" that you keep by your bed, but you must stay absolutely committed to recording the "joys" of your day every night before you go to sleep. As the days collect, you'll be able to pull on those memories as a reference point for the good that exists. Even in times that seem dire, finding one small moment of good will keep you on track.

- **Find someone who will hold you accountable.** It is so easy to get sucked into the drama of little moments that pull us away from the good. Knowing that you have a trusted friend or a coach who will keep you on track in that commitment is essential. It is OK to ask for help. In fact, asking for support is a necessity. While in high school, my grandma and I sent e-mails to each other every day sharing one joy. No matter what. Even if it was just a great cup of coffee. We were forced to share that joy, to find that one thing. Whether you do this in a physical book, in an e-mail, or even in a daily Instagram post (#spreadjoy #joyjournal365), building a community around your commitment will bring you back when you get off track.

- **Fill up!** I was once given an opportunity to speak with Daniel Day Lewis. I asked him how he suggested we balance our life with our career. He looked straight in my eyes (a.k.a. my soul) and said, "This career will scoop the life out of you. If you don't set aside time to fill up, you will not survive." That is true for performers as well as many others. If you are making a full-force commitment to giving good, to spreading joy, you must make time to fill up so that you have enough to give. You must be steadfast about committing to yourself and your own joy before you are able to give that goodness to the world.

- Recognize the joy that exists every day, and keep a record of it.

- Find someone who will hold you accountable and committed to recording the everyday joys.

- Make filling your own cup your top priority so that you are able to give to others.

On a Clear Day You Can See Forever

Do you remember being asked in high school to write out the life you saw yourself living as an adult? Was that fun and exciting, or did you feel awkward and uncertain?

As you got older and started thinking about dating or marriage, did you ever toy with the idea of filling out a dating profile? They make you answer all of these questions about who you want and what you want. Was that fun and exciting, or did you feel awkward, uncertain, and maybe a little embarrassed?

Now think back to when you woke up this morning. Were you aware of the day you wanted to have? The life you wanted to lead? Were you excited about attacking your day and making it happen? Or does that idea feel awkward, filled with uncertainty, and embarrassing?

Whether or not you realize it, you are mapping out the life you want to lead over and over again, all day, every day. If you don't know what you are heading toward, how can you make choices that will bring you closer to your dream life, your dream career, your dream partner?

Maybe it was fun and exciting for you to imagine your dream life as a kid. For most of us though, it's overwhelming. You might be embarrassed to really put it out there for fear of failure. You might feel guilty for wanting so much because of moments that your mind and heart have clung to that tell you that you don't deserve it. How sad, right?

I love helping my clients see their own possibility and get jazzed about a life filled with excitement and joy. When I realized that the character work I was doing with my acting students was highly applicable to *real life*, my mind was blown. These tools will help you get clear so that you can put a plan into action and start living the life *you* want to live today.

When you see an actor who seems to be living the life of their character, it looks effortless, specific, and clear. What you don't see is all the work that went into each moment that they're living. Most actors will identify their character's *objective* (what their character wants) and then identify specific *tactics* (ways for their character to get what they want). Answering the following questions about your own life will enable you to see a clear path and step onto your own stage.

1. WHAT IS YOUR OBJECTIVE?

You need a clear, focused objective at the forefront of every decision. All choices must filter up to that one specific target. I know simplifying your life to one solitary objective seems impossible, but when it comes down to it, for most people your clearest objective is bringing in more joy. Whether than means more time, more money, more energy, less stress ... you must start by connecting with your joy.

Start by looking at your joy journal and noticing the moments that make you the happiest. You might be surprised to find that you are happiest when you are reading a book, or cuddling with your two-year-old, or working out, or taking a nap, or painting, or knitting, or cooking, or connecting with others ... the list could go on and on. Get clear about what you want and what you don't want.

2. WHAT ARE YOUR TACTICS?

Tactics are active, specific ways you can bring more of what you want into your life. What is preventing you from experiencing that joy? I love what Todd Herman of The 90 Day Year says, "You don't have a problem; you have a choice." You are going to actively work to bring more joy into your life. Look at your calendar and see how you can make that joy a bigger part of your life.

If your calendar is overbooked, maybe you need to create more free time so that you can do what you love, or perhaps you need to find ways to incorporate your joy into everything that is in your calendar. If you have the time, maybe you need more money to do the things that bring you joy. Your tactic would be to increase your income or decrease your spending so that you have the ability to bring in more joy. If you have the time and the money, perhaps you just need to actually commit and make the change. Actively pursue the objective of spreading joy and take charge of your life, living the life you want to lead.

One thing I love about tactics is that there can be hundreds of them leading up to one main objective, so start making a list. Write down all the actions you can take toward bringing your specific objective to life. Revisit that list daily, and start putting those tactics into action.

3. SUPER OBJECTIVE

Once you become better at knowing what you want on a day-to-day basis, it's time to decide what you want in a grand way, a "super objective." For an actor, this is the difference between knowing what your character wants in a scene and knowing what they want over the course of an entire play. The better control you have over what you want on a small scale, the more plausible and exciting it will be to set your sights on the larger dream. And again, what really brings it into reality is taking that extra step and putting it out there, actually telling someone about it and having them help to hold you accountable.

This is what makes online dating so scary. You have to admit to others that you have dreams. That you deserve success. That you deserve joy. Well, guess what? You do! Keeping those dreams and desires hidden is a sure way to make certain they do not come into fruition.

So I challenge you to take action by following this plan:

- Take a week and commit daily to actively pursuing your simple daily joys.

- At the end of that week, take an hour to analyze what it felt like to put your joy first. Was it exciting? Was it scary? Do you want more of that joy?

- Write out what a life filled with that joy would include. Where are you living? Where are you working? Who surrounds you?

- Call a friend or a coach and tell them about it! Ask them to hold you accountable.

For example, I once coached someone who did this exercise and realized he was happiest when connecting with others; however, he had put himself in a work situation that kept him very isolated. So he made a simple shift and started to actively increase his plans with others.

Instead of eating alone because it was easy and convenient, he would make it a point to dine in a group. He started reaching out and scheduling time with those that were important to him. He made an effort to make more phone calls. About a week after making a list of ways he could actively bring more of his own joy into his life, he was blown away by how everything in his life had changed. It really is as simple as identifying what brings you joy and actively working toward bringing more of that goodness.

Your Instant Insights...

- When you discover what brings you joy, you are able to set clear, focused goals.

- When you bring in more of what you want on a small, day-to-day basis, your dreams become easier to visualize.

- Share your larger, lifelong aspirations with others. It's scary but exhilarating, and it will keep you on track.

Wear Like You Care

When you see someone in a blue gingham dress and red shoes, what comes to mind?

How about someone with a rolled-up denim shirt and a red bandana tied around the neck?

A blue shirt emblazoned with a red and yellow triangle?

A white, sparkly glove?

Hopefully at least one of those descriptions rang a bell. You should have thought of Dorothy, Rosie the Riveter, Superman, and Michael Jackson. Performers know that we make an impression as soon as we walk onto the stage. It's important to know the difference between being superficial and materialistic, and simply putting thought into your appearance. I always say that you should "wear like you care," and if you can make choices that also help create a recognizable brand, even better.

For some, this just comes naturally. They instinctively know what clothes they feel best in and how to present themselves in a manner that forces them to command attention as soon as they walk into a room. For some, it's a little overwhelming. For others, it's downright terrifying; the thought of worrying about what they are going to wear makes them miserable. No matter where you lie on that spectrum, these points will help you to own a room as soon as you walk through the door.

- **Bring "style" into your awareness.** As you go through your day, simply notice what you like and don't like about what others are wearing. We all have different tastes, and those tastes enable us to make a statement when we enter a room. Simply noticing what you connect (or don't connect) with will help you start to make a style statement of your own.

- **Connect your style choices to your joy.** Go back to that joy journal. Look over your list of things that make you uniquely awesome. See how you can incorporate that into your style choices.

For example, I have loved swing dancing since I was sixteen, and my favorite style choices always had a vintage feel. When I wear a pencil skirt, I carry myself in a completely different way than when I wear jeans.

My husband is *obsessed* with buttoning his top button on his shirts. We all joke about it, but it matches his personality perfectly. He loves everything to be in its place and wants everything to be used to its fullest extent. To see him with his shirt unbuttoned throws everything out of whack.

I have a client who loves the ocean, and we were talking about incorporating blue into her brand. If you love the ocean, incorporating that blue into your wardrobe could be a perfect choice for you.

Subtle additions to your clothing choices will not only boost your sense of confidence because it will fill you with joy, it will also help others connect with you and feel that joy as well.

- **Get feedback from a trusted friend or coach.** If this is putting you way out of your comfort zone, ask for help! Have you been on Facebook lately? Holy smokes! People love to give their opinions. Put together a few selections and see what people think, or if you aren't comfortable putting it out on social media, ask a friend. I would like to add, however, that it might be a good idea to avoid asking your spouse. I know this can get personal, and feelings are at risk of getting hurt. Find someone you know you can trust but with whom the stakes aren't too high.

- **Know that everyone has their own opinions, and you can take them or leave them.** Yes, it's great to get others' opinions, but if you feel awesome in something, who cares what others think! You will weed out those who aren't brave enough to embrace their own spotlight, and you'll bring in those who are ready to celebrate.

- **Accessorize with intentional simplicity.** Coco Chanel once said, "Before leaving the house, a lady should look in the mirror and remove one accessory." I love to ensure that my accessories have great meaning. However, wearing them all at once will give your "audience" a headache. They'll have no idea where to focus.

When you are choosing your accessories, think of an objective. How do you want others to feel when they see you walk into a room? Do you want them to know you are powerful and mean business? Do you want to seem approachable? Do you want them to know you are ready to play?

I have a pair of pink and blue John Fluevog shoes that always spark a conversation. Honestly, every time I wear them someone comes up and talks to me, so I intentionally wear them to events where I'm looking to connect with others. One of my young students calls them my "shoes that help me make friends." Conversely, if I am heading out to a coffee shop where I intend to bury my head in my computer and get work done, my objective is quite the opposite. I would instead wear simple muted shoes that help me to blend in.

You don't need to spend loads of money on accessories in order to make a statement. One of my favorite places to find treasures that I know will help me light up a room is T.J. Maxx. I'm a full-fledged "Maxxinista." Places like T.J. Maxx or Nordstrom Rack often have amazing, affordable finds for both men and women. You never know when the right piece that will help you make the right statement will jump out at you; be open to the idea, and your statement piece will find its way to you.

- **Hair like you care.** Your hair can also help you make an instant statement and have a major effect on your confidence level. If you've ever attended one of my events or seen my videos, you might have noticed that I incorporate a subtle hidden flair in my hair. I often have peek-a-boo peacock colors died under the top layer. I've even incorporated this style choice into my logo, which includes a cartoon version of me who has turquoise highlights. (She was designed by my good friend and graphic designer Melissa Cullen.)   However, my hairstylist Amber Pfeifer knows that I'm not in a position to have a full head of blue hair like many artists.   When I walk into a meeting with a corporate client, I'm not always sure if blue hair is going to be acceptable, and I want to respect that, so I wear my hair in a manner that keeps the colors hidden until I've felt out my audience. I always want to be able to turn the party on in the flip of a second, so once I know what type of crowd I'm dealing with, I can let my party side out by simply tossing my hair. It's like magic! (There is also a world of fun to be played with in your nails and makeup! So play!)

- **Know your audience.** We all play in different theaters with different limitations. You must know your own quesadilla recipe, your objective, and who you are speaking to in order to give off the perfect impression. It is a delicate balance for sure, but once you start to play, it's a liberating blast!

- **Set strategic limitations.** Man, I love this tip! Once you start to feel a little free with your choices, you might go on a frenzy and take it a little too far. That's OK! But you don't want to suffer from decision fatigue (it's a real thing—Google it) because you have so many amazing options. It's good to set some boundaries when it comes to your wardrobe. In fact, many of the most successful people swear by this idea, including President Barack Obama who told *Vanity Fair*, "You'll see I wear only gray or blue suits. I'm trying to pare down decisions. I don't want to make decisions about what I'm eating or wearing. Because I have too many other decisions to make."

I also love what Alice Gregory had to say in her piece for J.Crew about the idea of wearing a uniform. She said, "[It is] iconic. A cheap and easy way to feel famous. A uniform can be a way of performing maturity or, less charitably, impersonating it." She also stated, "This is the reason why characters in picture books never change their clothes: Children—like adults, if they'd only admit it—crave continuity."

Look at Steve Jobs and his black turtleneck. It not only made him a recognizable figure, it helped define the Apple brand itself— sleek and simple. You might not need to go that far, but paring down to a few colors or styles will bring simplicity and can allow you to expand creatively in other ways.

Like many women, I've recently developed an obsession with the clothing line Lularoe. It has helped me incorporate so much joy into my wardrobe and forced simplicity. I just choose from among leggings, a pencil skirt, or a 50s dress with pockets, and I'm good to go! I love it so much that I've even started hosting a pop-up shop on Wednesdays with a new consultant once a week. It's a great way to support these awesome businesswomen and share their goodness with others. You can check it out at www.ThePreparedPerformer.com/wtw.

Your Instant Insights...

- Start to be aware of how the style choices of those around you affect you. As your awareness is heightened, you'll start to know the best choices for you! You'll be better suited to "wear like you care."

- Connect your style to your joy! Your appearance is another great way to commit to cultivating and spreading joy.

- Set strategic limitations on your wardrobe and style choices. When you set limitations, you open up more doors for creative freedom and give others a way to identify you. You become your brand.

The Show Must Go On

Do you ever wonder how performers always manage to muster up the energy to put on a fabulous show? Sometimes they perform three or four times in one day ... while on tour ... where they are sleeping on a bus! A fierce amount of discipline and drive is mandatory, or the show will not go on. When you have an audience filled with hundreds of people, there's no other option. The Show Must Go On.

Many nonperformers think is easy. You love what you do, so you just get up with a pep in your step, right? No way! It's hard—like, really hard. When I work with performers, a huge portion of what I do is help them summon the courage to keep going after an audition, or an injury, or just being tired because it's so much work.

Here are seven key factors that will change your energy and your outlook so that you can walk into your day as if you are walking onto a Broadway stage. (At the end of this chapter, I share my secret weapon for staying on track.)

1. **Set a clear objective, and know why you are working toward that objective.** Don't just think about it—write it down. Commit, and know why you are committing. When you wake up and feel that ping of "Ugh, just five more minutes," or when you are afraid to hit send on an e-mail quoting a price that is out of your comfort zone, or if you start to throw the towel in because you just can't handle another rejection, think about your objective and *why* you have chosen to commit to it. If you have a strong enough *why*, you'll push through the difficult, uncomfortable times.

2. **Plan your tactics, and put them in your calendar, including prep time and wrap-up time.** A performer's job never starts when the lights go up on the stage. There is always a "call time" at least a half hour before the actual show. It's built in; no questions asked. Installing that same buffer will allow you to take a moment to prepare, and a buffer at the end is just as important. A performer has a buffer at the end of each show to get out of costume, reset props, and close up shop. Heck,

sometimes I'd just sit there for a moment after my shows so that I could breathe for a second. You need time to wrap up, to wind down.

3. **Nap intentionally.** People often ask me if I ever sleep. I know they are joking (most of the time), but honestly, sometimes I don't want to sleep because there is so much good to be experienced in this world—I don't want to miss it. Once you've fully connected to your joy, your why, and your objective, you might feel this way too. Napping intentionally is an amazingly effective trick that I learned from my friend Adam Pliska, president of the World Poker Tour. I so clearly remember being in my early twenties and learning that he had a spot dedicated to napping in his office. At first, I was amused, but it's actually one of the best bits of advice I've received. Give yourself twenty minutes, and set your intention on rejuvenating rest.

4. **When you start to feel really overwhelmed and tired, make a change**. Seriously. If something is getting in the way of your joy, don't allow yourself to sit in the misery. Analyze the situation and *change*.

5. **Set aside time for fun.** If you are fully giving your all to your objective, you need to fill up! Remember that Daniel Day

Lewis quote? He was referring to the crazy life of a performer, but the advice goes for anything that you are wholeheartedly committed to! If you aren't careful, a wholehearted commitment to anything can scoop the life out of you. Take a break and play!

6. **Move!** Speaking of taking a break and playing, stretch, strengthen, and stride down the street. I don't care how you do it, but make sure you set aside time to moooooooove in addition to everything else you are working toward. Who was it that said, "A body in motion stays in motion"? Was it Dory from *Finding Nemo*? Oh no, she said, "Just keep swimming. Just keep swimming!" It wasn't Dory; it was Isaac Newton. But they're saying the same thing! I can guarantee that nothing will change if you stay still. Get up and *move*.

7. **Drink Water.** I know ... it sounds silly. You hear this all the time. It's sooooo simple! But do you do it? Probably not as often as you should. I find that adding some sort of fizzy vitamin mixture to my water makes me more inclined to drink it more often. There are apps that help you remember, or you can set a timer or a calendar event! Do. It.

My Secret Weapon for Staying on Task: The Magic Feather

This really is my secret weapon. If you choose wisely, it will have a huge impact on your ability to stay the course. Remember watching the movie *Dumbo* as a child? What happened? He fell asleep on a branch, and he woke up surrounded by crows in the branch of a tall tree. "What!?" he thinks. "How did I get up here?" That's when he realizes that he must have flown up there. Whoa, what? He did not know he had the power to fly. Then of course he gets afraid because he didn't believe he was actually that powerful. So those crows give him the magic feather and that magic feather gives him the power to fly! He's a magical elephant because he has this **magic feather.**

Then, right before he's ready to fly in front of the whole entire circus, he loses the magic feather. In a freaked-out panic, he jumps, and he realizes he was always a magical elephant. He didn't need the magic feather; the power was within him. He was able to fly all along, but that magic feather gave him that extra boost of confidence.

You are going to find your magic feather—a physical object. You don't need to go buy anything; this can be something that you already own. You're going to use this physical thing to help remind you of your "why," to help keep you on track. Making change is hard. Striving for new, amazing objectives and dreams is hard! It's so easy to say, "Nope, I'm not doing it anymore," to just turn off and say, "I'll get to it later. I'll get to it later."

Here are a few ideas. If there's a ring that you have that you wear every once in a while but you can give it the power to hold you accountable, put it on like the Green Lantern has his magical ring. Or there's Jem from Jem and the Holograms. She has her earrings, and she channels this energy through her earrings. I have a pair of bright pink and blue John Fluevog shoes that change my energy every time I wear them to an event. They say, "Yes! I mean business. I'm on my mission to connect with as many people as possible." The shoes are crazy and often people will come up to me and say, "Oh my gosh, I love your shoes!" They now work as a magic feather to remind myself to connect with others. Your magic feather doesn't even have to be something that you wear. You could paint your fingernails a certain color or change the color of your cell-phone case. A physical item that you can see and feel will really help bring you back on track.

Your Instant Insights...

- Knowing what you are working toward and exactly why you are working toward it gives you a reason to take the next step, especially when you are faced with rejection and fear.

- When you accomplish something, celebrate! Accept each win as a reason to party, then get back to work!

- Create or identify a magic feather, a small tactile object that will keep you on course.

Take That Show on the Road

You've now made a huge list of the things that make you an awesome person. You are celebrating the awesome in yourself and in others. You have committed to connecting with and insisting on more joy in your life. You've done work to find clarity in your objectives and the tactics it takes to get there. And you are starting to use the tricks performers have used for ages to bring more energy and focus into your life when you need it most, ensuring that "The Show Must Go On!"

Now what? How do you "take your show on the road"?

While I was on the Broadway national tour of *Chitty Chitty Bang Bang*, I learned the number-one secret to a successful touring production: a company manager. This person not only ensures that every company member (cast, crew, and musician) has a flight, a hotel room, a seat on the bus or a rental car, and a list of all the necessary phone numbers and addresses nearby, they are also responsible for keeping up the morale of the company members, for setting the tone so that the company gets along, feels taken care of, and continues to bring their best to the production night after night.

How amazing would it be to have your own company manager who ran your business and your life? In this last chapter, I show you how to secretly create your own company manager so that you can focus on the thing that is most important: cultivating and spreading your joy!

This is going to take a little prep work, but once you get into the habit of following these steps, it will work itself. To help you, I've created a downloadable worksheet that you can get for FREE at www.PerformancePowerBook.com/plan.

- **Pick a singular objective that will help bring more joy into your life or business.** Sounds familiar, right? But it's so important.

- **Be sure you know why you are pursuing this objective.** (This should be easy by now!) Write it down, and tell someone about it!

- **Take that objective and set one specific goal that you can accomplish within two weeks.** So often we set yearlong goals at the top of the year, but did you know that most professional theaters rehearse for only two weeks? Yep. They rehearse for two weeks and then have a week of technical rehearsals before opening the full-blown show in front of an audience. Crazy, right? Crazy, but awesome! I love setting mini two-week goals so that there is time to review and adjust. It's much easier to get something done when you are focused on one thing, rather than splitting your time among several projects.

- **Take that goal and list all the steps needed to get it done.** Literally write it all out. This will be different for everyone and for every project. Whether you are helping plan a fundraiser for your daughter's dance studio or planning on launching a podcast, there are loads of little steps that go into completing the project. Often, we underestimate the amount of work that goes into the projects we take on. Writing it all out will help you understand all that is ahead of you, and it will help you to eventually pass the project on to others.

- **Set a specific date and time for every task (no matter how small).** While a paper or digital calendar is great for this (and super necessary), I've recently fallen in love with a tool called Asana that helps map out every detail of a project. You can visit www.PerformancePowerBook.com/asana to see my tutorial on this tool and learn more. It enables you to list all your projects and divide them into tasks with specific due dates. Then you can assign those tasks to yourself so that you are sent an e-mail reminder, or you can assign the tasks to members of your team so that they will be sent a reminder and can mark the task as complete.

- **Set aside specific *you* time to fill up.** This time for you is a necessity, just like breathing. When you prioritize *you*, you'll have more to give to the other people and organizations that need you most.

- **If you don't actually have time to accomplish these tasks, assess your schedule, and see what you can delegate**. Is it time to hire an assistant? A housekeeper? A nanny? If your objective is powerful enough, it may be time to ask for help. (Pssst! Most company managers have assistants.)

- **Bring out that magic feather, and allow it to serve as a sweet little reminder to**

stay on task. This trick is so powerful. It's very easy to allow yourself to stray away from your goal. If you can't think of something you could wear or keep with you to serve as a reminder, try changing up something subtle that you do every day. If you have a habit of putting on the left shoe and then the right, try putting on the "other" shoe first.

- **Set a specific time each week to review your progress.** If there is a task that you did not complete, identify why you didn't complete it. Is it worth adding to your plan for the next two weeks? Should you let it go? **Decide.** If there are tasks that you have completed ... celebrate! These two-week goals are so beneficial. It's like a mini New Year's Eve every two weeks!

- **Make your calendar your boss!** Seriously. No questions asked. (This one is haaaaard.) When you are in charge of your own life, you'll find great freedom, and you'll realize that it's easy to let things slip through the cracks. So you need a clear calendar system. You can use a paper calendar, a large wall calendar, a digital calendar (my favorite is the basic Google calendar)—some sort of calendar that you can obey as the one in charge.

- **Talk to a friend or a coach about this new plan, and ask them to hold you**

accountable. Changes like this can be overwhelming and scary. Having a support system will accelerate the process and multiply the good!

Following the steps in this list will drastically change the way you accomplish your goals, but you have to follow them all! If you let one of these steps slip through the cracks, you'll find yourself either overwhelmed or left behind. I know it can seem overwhelming. I know it's easy to let things slide when you are in control of your own life. But, hey! That is why the reward is so sweet. You are *awesome*!

Your Instant Insights...

- Setting two-week goals for yourself is much more effective than long-term goals because you can review, adjust, and keep moving forward.

- Write down all the steps it takes to finish a specific task. It can be hard to justify setting aside time to record a process, but it will help you streamline and make it easier when it comes time to pass tasks off to others on your team.

- If you can't fit all that you want to accomplish into your week, cut back, or ask for help.

Acknowledgements

Thank you to the Bagillions of coaches and teachers who have helped me to craft the core message and teachings of The Prepared Performer, including but not limited to... Mom, Dad, Mary, John, Grandparents, Aunts and Uncles, teachers at The Music Room School of Performing Arts, professors and Chapman University, Cyrus Parker-Jeannette, Andrew M. Byrne, Chloe Wing, Dana Corey, Dana Rich, Dawnmarie Presley, Debbie Whitlock, Chellie Campbell, the members of the eWomenNetwork, The Chance Theater, Robbin Simons and the Crescendo Team, Anthony Boyer, Morgan Crane and my crazy beautiful, hardworking y-sisters, John Dominguez, Frank, and Charleston Dominguez, and the crazy brave and amazing Prepared Performers.

About the Author

Molly Mahoney, a proud member of the Actors Equity Association, earned a bachelor of fine arts in theatre and dance performance from Chapman University. She has spent the past ten years performing in regional theaters across the country and in NYC jazz clubs, aboard cruise ships, and in Las Vegas at The Rio Hotel and Casino. She has a full-length CD of original music entitled *Get What You're After* (now available on iTunes). You can also spot her swing dancing in the dance-marathon episode of *Gilmore Girls*, "They Shoot Gilmores, Don't They?" directed by Kenny Ortega. Maybe you saw her in your hometown while she performed with the national tour of *Chitty Chitty Bang Bang*, While working as a professional performer, Molly has been lucky enough to study with legends Henry Le Tang, Frankie Manning, Fayard Nicholas of the Nicholas Brothers, and her favorite tap guru Ray Hesselink. She has studied voice with Andrew Byrne and Joann Zajac, acting with John Ruocco and Joan Rosenfels, and Alexander Technique with Chloe Wing.

After working consistently as a performer out of NYC for several years, she now loves sharing all that she learned in order to help her students and clients attack their goals with clarity, confidence, and joy. Molly shows business owners and their teams how to bring a sense of stage presence to their everyday lives. When not celebrating the goodness of her clients, she loves cuddling her boys, who are four and two years old, and singing with her bass-playing husband.

Molly believes learning to dance, act, and sing as a child has enriched her life in ways she could have never imagined, and she loves sharing her enthusiasm with her students.

Connect with the Author

Website:
www.ThePreparedPerformer.com

Email:
Molly@ThePreparedPerformer.com

Social Media:
Facebook: www.Facebook.com/
thepreparedperformer

LinkedIn:
www.ThePreparedPerformer.com/linkedin

Twitter: @Prep2Perform

Instagram: ThePreparedPerformer

Periscope: ThePreparedPerformer

Snapchat: PreparedPerform

Pinterest: https://www.pinterest.com/molly_m_
mahoney/the-prepared-performer/

Google+ ThePreparedPerformer

Address:
1833 N. Shaffer St. Orange, CA 92865

About Crescendo Publishing

Crescendo Publishing is a boutique-style, concierge VIP publishing company assisting entrepreneurs with writing, publishing, and promoting their books for the purposes of lead-generation and achieving global platform growth, then monetizing it for even more income opportunities.

Check out some of our latest best-selling AuthorPreneurs at http://CrescendoPublishing. com/new-authors/.

About the Instant Insights™ Book Series

The *Instant Insights™ Book Series* is a fact-only, short-read, book series written by EXPERTS in very specialized categories. These high-value, high-quality books can be produced in ONLY 6-8 weeks, from concept to launch, in BOTH PRINT & eBOOK Formats!

This book series is FOR YOU if:

- You are an expert in your niche or area of specialty

- You want to write a book to position yourself as an expert

- You want YOUR OWN book – NOT a chapter in someone else's book

- You want to have a book to give to people when you're speaking at events or simply networking

- You want to have it available quickly

- You don't have the time to invest in writing a 200-page full book

- You don't have a ton of money to invest in the production of a full book – editing, cover design, interior layout, best-seller promotion

- You don't have a ton of time to invest
  in finding quality contractors for the
  production of your book – editing,
  cover design, interior layout, best-seller
  promotion

For more information on how you can become
an *Instant Insights™* author,
visit **www.InstantInsightsBooks.com**

More Books in the
Instant Insight™ Series

CrescendoPublishing.com

Made in the USA
San Bernardino, CA
18 April 2017